# DEEPAK CHOPRA

❖ ABRIDGED EDITION ❖

# THE SEVEN SPIRITUAL LAWS OF SUCCESS

A POCKETBOOK GUIDE TO
FULFILLING YOUR DREAMS

AMBER-ALLEN PUBLISHING
SAN RAFAEL, CALIFORNIA

• ONE HOUR OF WISDOM •

Published by Amber-Allen Publishing, Inc.
P.O. Box 6657
San Rafael, CA 94903

Cover art: *Asavari Ragini*, Subimperial Mughal, c. 1625

**Library of Congress Cataloging-in-Publication Data**
Chopra, Deepak.
The seven spiritual laws of success : a pocketbook guide
to fulfilling your dreams / Deepak Chopra. -- Abridged ed.
p. cm. --  (One hour of wisdom)
ISBN  978-1-878424-60-0
1. Success in business--Religious aspects. 2. Success--
Religious aspects. 3. Wealth--Psychological aspects. I. Title.
HF5386.C5475 2007
650.1--dc22                                      2007014211

Printed in Canada on acid-free paper
Distributed by Hay House, Inc.
10  9  8  7  6  5  4  3  2  1

To Janet Mills, with gratitude for bringing
this manuscript to completion.

# CONTENTS

⋘⋙

*Books are infinite in number, and time is short;
therefore the secret of knowledge is to take what is
essential. Take that and try to live up to it.*
— Swami Vivekananda

## NOTE FROM THE PUBLISHER ON
## "ONE HOUR OF WISDOM"

Inspiration is a wonderful gift to give ourselves each day. To nurture our spirit, to be reminded of the power of life flowing through us, to be inspired to manage our power with greater awareness — this is the purpose of "One Hour of Wisdom." Most of us spend more time taking care of our material possessions than we spend taking care of our spirit. In a world where so many things require our attention, the larger purpose of our lives can be forgotten. This book captures the essence of the author's wisdom, and shares a wealth of information in less time than it takes to prepare ourselves a meal.

Words and ideas can heal the mind and nurture the soul. Words are alive with energy; they have the power to uplift, to enliven, to transform. Feel the energy of the words in these pages as you read them; intend for the gift of their wisdom to be received.

Life is a force flowing through us. Where we direct our attention, is where our life force flows. Every moment is an opportunity to direct our attention to ideas that inspire us.

Every day brings the promise of a new beginning, and the opportunity to transform every life challenge into a gift. One hour, one idea, one act of love can make all the difference.

There is an art to living with joy, and a science to managing all forms of energy, including our own. Learning to manage the force of life flowing through us is a worthy endeavor, and one that brings many rewards.

May this book help you to see yourself with greater clarity. May its wisdom help you to express all the power of your spirit, and to fulfill your most cherished dreams. Perhaps you will read this book in less than one hour, but if you read it again and again, the essence of its wisdom will linger for a lifetime.

*The ancient sages described the most effortless way
to bond with the universe and fulfill our desires.
Their guiding motto turns out to be exquisitely simple:
Act in accord with the laws of nature.*
— Deepak Chopra

## INTRODUCTION

This book is titled *The Seven Spiritual Laws of Success*, but it could also be called *The Seven Spiritual Laws of Life*, because these are the same principles that nature uses to create everything in material existence — everything we can see, hear, smell, taste, or touch. When this knowledge is incorporated in our consciousness, it gives us the ability to create unlimited wealth with effortless ease, and to experience success in every endeavor.

Success in life can be defined as the continued expansion of happiness and the progressive realization of worthy goals. There are many aspects to success; material wealth is only one of them. Moreover, success is a journey, not a destination. Material abundance, in all its expressions, happens to make the journey more enjoyable, but success includes good health, energy and enthusiasm for life, fulfilling relationships, creative freedom, and a sense of well-being.

Success is the ability to fulfill our desires with effortless ease. And yet success, including the creation of wealth, has always been considered to be a process that requires hard work, and it is often considered to be at the expense of others. We need a more spiritual approach to success and to affluence, which is the abundant flow of all good things to us.

In spiritual terms, success is measured by how efficiently, how effortlessly, we co-create with the universe. Hard work, struggle, and frustration are the opposite of what the ancient sages taught; they knew that spirit lies at the source of all achievement in life. They always began at the source, and they defined the source as pure potentiality, which is purely unmanifest consciousness. The beauty of beginning at the source is that power resides there — the power of our inner being, the power of our spirit.

In every seed lies the promise of a forest. Unseen energy flows into material manifestation. The physical laws of the universe are actually the process by which the unmanifest, unknown, and invisible is transformed into the manifest, known, and visible. Our most cherished desires are pure consciousness seeking expression from the unmanifest to the manifest. And if we give our deeper instincts a chance, success in life is not only possible, but inevitable.

With the knowledge and practice of the seven spiritual laws, we align with nature's intelligence, and our dreams and desires are easily fulfilled. When we understand these laws, and apply them in our lives, anything we want can be created.

# 1

## THE LAW OF
## PURE POTENTIALITY

*In the beginning there was neither existence nor nonexistence. All this world was unmanifest energy....*
*--Hymn of Creation, The Rig Veda*

# 1

## THE LAW OF
## PURE POTENTIALITY

The first spiritual law of success, the *Law of Pure Potentiality*, says that our essential state is one of pure potentiality. Pure potentiality is pure consciousness; it is the field of all possibilities and infinite creativity. Our physical body, the physical universe — everything in the material world — comes from the same place: a field of silent, unmoving awareness from which anything is possible. There is no separation between this field of energy and our spiritual essence, our Self. This field *is* our own Self. And when we know that our essential nature is one of pure potentiality, we align with the power that manifests everything in the universe.

Knowing who we really are gives us the ability to fulfill any dream we have, because the same field that nature uses to create a forest, a galaxy, or a human body can also bring about the fulfillment of our desires. Anything is possible in the field of pure potentiality, because this field is the *source* of all power, all intelligence, and infinite organizing ability.

Therefore, success in life depends on knowing who we really are. When our internal reference point is our spirit, our *true* Self, we experience all the power of our spirit. When our internal reference point is the ego or self-image, we feel cut off from our source, and the uncertainty of events creates fear and doubt. The ego is influenced by objects outside the Self — circumstances, people, and things. It thrives on the approval of others. It wants to control, because it lives in fear. But the ego is not who we really are. The ego is our social mask; it is the role we are playing.

The need for approval, the need to control things, and the need for external power are fear based. This kind of power is not the power of pure potentiality, the power of the Self, or *true* power. Self-power is true power because it is based on the laws of nature, and comes from knowledge of the Self. Self-power draws things that we want to us; it magnetizes people, situations, and things to support our desires. This support from the laws of nature is the state of grace. When we are in harmony with nature, we create a bond between our own desires and the power to make these desires materialize.

How can you experience the *Law of Pure Potentiality*? One way is through the practice of silence and meditation. This means tuning out the world and taking time to simply *Be*.

THE LAW OF PURE POTENTIALITY

In the Bible is the expression "Be still, and know that I am God." Stillness is the first requirement for manifesting your desires, because in stillness you connect with the field of pure awareness and infinite organizing power.

Imagine throwing a little stone into a still pond and watching it ripple. That's what you do when you go into silence and introduce your intention. Even the faintest intention ripples across the field of universal consciousness that connects your desire with everything else. This field can orchestrate an infinity of details for you. But if your mind is like a turbulent ocean, you could throw the Empire State Building into it and you wouldn't notice a thing.

Practicing nonjudgment is another way to experience the *Law of Pure Potentiality.* When you are constantly judging things as right or wrong, good or bad, you create a lot of turbulence in your internal dialogue. This turbulence constricts the flow of energy between you and the field of pure potentiality. In the silent space between your thoughts is a state of pure awareness, an inner stillness that connects you to true power. Through the practice of nonjudgment, you silence your mind and access your inner stillness.

Another way to experience the *Law of Pure Potentiality* is to spend time in nature. By observing nature you begin to sense the harmonious interaction of all the elements and forces of life. The lavish display of abundance in the universe is an expression of the creative mind of nature. Just by tuning in to the mind of nature, you will access the field of pure potentiality and infinite creativity, and spontaneously receive creative thoughts.

Whether it be a stream, a forest, a mountain, or the sea, connecting with nature's intelligence will give you a sense of unity with all of life, and help you to get in touch with the innermost essence of your being. This essence is full of magic and mystery. It is fearless; it is free. When you are grounded in the knowledge of your true Self, you never feel fearful or insecure about money or fulfilling your desires. You never feel guilty about wanting or having an abundance of anything, because you realize that the essence of all material wealth is life energy. You know that your desires are inseparably connected with everything else. Your very desire is not your own; it's an evolutionary impulse coming through you, so why would you doubt it? That impulse is part of the greater pattern, which is to grow and evolve into greater abundance and creativity.

The *Law of Pure Potentiality* says that you are consciousness itself, both as it manifests in the material world, and as it lies unmanifest in your being. With the knowledge and practice of this law, you can put yourself in harmony with nature and create with carefreeness, joy, and love. Wherever you go in the midst of activity, carry your stillness within you. Then the chaotic activity around you will never overshadow your access to the field of pure potentiality.

To experience the *Law of Pure Potentiality*:

❖ Take time each day to be silent, to connect with your spirit, to just *Be*.

❖ Practice nonjudgment. Begin each day with the statement "Today, I shall judge nothing that occurs," and throughout the day remind yourself of that statement each time you catch yourself judging.

❖ Commune with nature. Silently observe the intelligence within everything. Watch a sunset, listen to the sound of the ocean, or simply smell the scent of a flower.

# 2

## THE LAW OF
## GIVING AND RECEIVING

*Thy infinite gifts come to me only on those very small hands of mine. Ages pass, and still thou pourest, and still there is room to fill.*
— Rabindranath Tagore, Gitanjali

# 2

# THE LAW OF
# GIVING AND RECEIVING

The second spiritual law of success, the *Law of Giving and Receiving*, is based on the fact that everything in the universe operates through dynamic exchange. Every relationship is one of give and take because giving and receiving are different aspects of the flow of energy in the universe. If we stop the flow of energy, we interfere with nature's intelligence. We must give and receive in order to keep money, or anything we want, circulating in our lives.

*Currency*, our word for money, derives from a Latin word meaning "to run or flow." Money is a symbol of the life energy we give and the life energy we receive as a result of the service we provide to others. Like a river, money must keep flowing; otherwise it begins to clog and stagnate. Circulation keeps it alive and vital. If we stop the circulation of life energy, if our intention is to hold on to our money and hoard it, we stop its circulation back into our lives.

The intention behind our giving and receiving is the most important thing. When

the act of giving is joyful, when it is uncon-
ditional and from the heart, then the energy
behind the giving increases many times over.
But if we give grudgingly, there is no energy
behind that giving. If we feel we have lost
something through the act of giving, then
the gift is not truly given and will not cause
increase.

The *Law of Giving and Receiving* is simple.
If you want love, learn to give love; if you
want attention and appreciation, learn to
give attention and appreciation; if you want
material affluence, help others to become
materially affluent. If you want to be blessed
with all the good things in life, learn to
silently bless everyone with all the good
things in life. The more you give, the more

you will receive. In your willingness to give that which you seek, you will keep the abundance of the universe circulating in your life.

Abundance has material expression, but what is really circulating is consciousness. Even the thought of giving, the thought of blessing, or a simple prayer has the power to affect others. We are bundles of thought in a thinking universe, and thought has the power to transform.

❧

The best way to experience the *Law of Giving and Receiving* is to give a gift to everyone you come into contact with. This doesn't have to be in the form of material things. The gifts of caring, affection, appreciation, and love are some of the most precious gifts you can give, and they don't cost you anything.

One of the things I was taught as a child is never to go to anyone's house without bringing a gift. You may say, "How can I give to others when I don't have enough myself?" You can bring a note that says something about your feelings for the person you're visiting. You can bring a flower, a compliment, or a prayer.

Whenever you meet someone, silently send that person a blessing. This kind of silent giving is very powerful. Give wherever you go, and as you give, you will receive. As you receive, the more your ability to give will increase, and the more you'll gain confidence in the miraculous effects of this law.

There is nothing you lack, because your essential nature is one of pure potentiality and infinite possibilities. You are inherently affluent no matter how much or how little money you have, because the source of all wealth is the field of pure potentiality that knows how to fill every need.

Giving and receiving are nothing other than the flow of life — the harmonious inter-action of all the elements and forces that structure the field of existence. The exchange of energy is a process that has its own timing, organization, and beauty. Your life unfolds in the same way. Everything that comes to you isn't something you earn, but a gift freely given by the universe, which means it comes from a deep awareness of what you need.

THE LAW OF GIVING AND RECEIVING

Think of all the things that have been freely given to you without your having to ask for them. Just experiencing gratitude allows you to participate in the *Law of Giving and Receiving*. Nature supports your every need and desire, including your need for joy, love, laughter, harmony, and knowledge. Seek these things first — not only for yourself, but for others — and all else will spontaneously come to you.

To experience the *Law of Giving and Receiving*.

❖ Give a gift to everyone you encounter, be it a compliment, a flower, or a prayer. This will begin the process of circulating joy and affluence in your life and in the lives of others.

❖ Gratefully receive every gift that life offers you. Be open to receiving, whether it be a material gift from others, a compliment, or a prayer.

❖ Silently wish everyone you encounter happiness, joy, and laughter. By giving and receiving the gifts of caring, affection, appreciation, and love, you will keep wealth circulating in your life.

# 3

## THE LAW OF KARMA
### OR CAUSE AND EFFECT

*Karma is the eternal assertion of human freedom....*
*Our thoughts, our words, and deeds are the threads*
*of the net which we throw around ourselves.*
*— Swami Vivekananda*

# 3

# THE LAW OF KARMA
# OR CAUSE AND EFFECT

The third spiritual law of success is the *Law of Karma* or *Cause and Effect*. Karma is both action and the consequence of that action. Everyone has heard the expression "What you sow is what you reap." If we want to create happiness in our lives, we must learn to sow the seeds of happiness.

Therefore, the *Law of Karma* implies the action of conscious choice making. When we choose actions that bring happiness and success to others, the fruit of our karma is happiness and success.

In every moment, we have access to an infinity of choices. Some choices are made consciously, while others are made unconsciously. Unfortunately, a lot of our choices are made unconsciously, and therefore we don't think they are choices — and yet, they are. As a result of conditioning, our choices are often triggered by people and circumstances into predictable outcomes.

If I were to insult you, you would most likely make the choice of being offended. If I were to pay you a compliment, you would most likely make the choice of being flattered. But think about it: You could make the choice of not being offended by an insult; you could make the choice of not letting a compliment flatter you either.

The best way to use karmic law is to step back and witness the choices you are making in every moment. When you make any choice, ask yourself two things: "What are the consequences of this choice?" and "Will the choice I'm making bring happiness to me and to those around me?" There is always one choice that will create maximum happiness both for you and for those around you. This choice is the spontaneous right action because it's the action that nourishes you and everyone else who is influenced by that action.

How do you make spontaneous right choices? By paying attention to sensations of comfort or discomfort in your body. At the moment you make a choice, ask your body, "What are the consequences of this choice?" If your body sends a message of comfort, that's the right choice. If you feel uneasiness in your body even as you ask the question, then it's not the appropriate choice.

For some people, the message of comfort or discomfort is in the area of the solar plexus, but for most people, it's in the area of the heart. Put your attention on your heart, and ask your heart what to do. Then pay attention to how you feel. The response may be the faintest level of feeling, but it's there. You will know the answer is right because it will *feel* right, without any lingering doubts. The heart knows the correct answer because it taps into the field of pure potentiality and infinite organizing power, and takes everything into account. The heart is intuitive and holistic; it has a win-win orientation. And though the answer may not seem rational, the heart is far more accurate than anything within the realm of rational thought.

You can use the *Law of Karma* to create money and the flow of all good things to you. But first, become aware of the choices that you are making in every moment. The more you become aware of your choices, the more you will make choices that are spontaneously correct — both for you and for those around you.

❧

How can you apply the *Law of Karma* to the choices you've already made? Most people pay their karmic debts — unconsciously, of course. Sometimes there's a lot of suffering involved, but the *Law of Karma* says no debt in the universe ever goes unpaid.

If you want to transform your karma to a more desirable experience, look for the seed of opportunity within every adversity, and tie that seed of opportunity to your *dharma*, or purpose in life. This will enable you to convert the adversity into a benefit, and transform the karma into a new expression.

Begin by asking yourself, "What message is the universe giving me? What can I learn from this experience, and how can I make it useful to my fellow human beings?" For example, if you break your leg while playing sports, perhaps the message is that you need to slow down and be more attentive to your body. And if your purpose in life is to teach others, then by asking, "What can I learn from this experience, and how can I make it useful to my fellow human beings?" you may decide to share what you've learned by writing a book about playing sports safely. This transforms your karma into a positive experience.

You can also transcend the seeds of your karma by becoming independent of it. The way to do this is to keep experiencing the Self, your spirit, by going into silent meditation and coming out again. This is like

THE SEVEN SPIRITUAL LAWS OF SUCCESS

washing a dirty piece of cloth in a stream of water. Each time you wash it, you take away a few stains, and it gets a little cleaner.

Every action is a karmic episode because action generates memory, memory generates desire, and desire generates action again. As you become conscious of these seeds of manifestation, you become a conscious choice maker, and the actions you generate will be evolutionary. As long as karma is evolutionary — both for you and for those around you — then the fruit of karma will be happiness and success.

To experience the *Law of Karma*:

❖ Witness the choices you make in every moment. The best way to prepare for any moment in the future is to be fully conscious in the present.

❖ Whenever you make a choice, ask yourself two questions: "What are the consequences of this choice?" and "Will this choice bring happiness to me and to those who are affected by this choice?"

❖ Ask your heart for guidance, and be guided by its message of comfort or discomfort. If the choice feels comfortable, go ahead with that choice. If the choice feels uncomfortable, then don't make that choice.

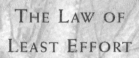

# 4
## ❦
# THE LAW OF
# LEAST EFFORT

# 4

## THE LAW OF
## LEAST EFFORT

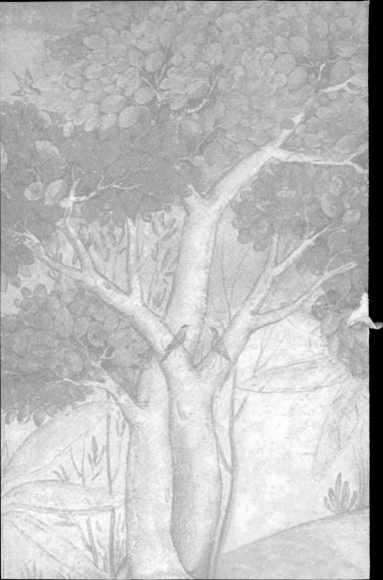

*An integral being knows without going, sees without looking, and accomplishes without doing.*
— Lao Tzu

# 4

## THE LAW OF
## LEAST EFFORT

The fourth spiritual law of success, the *Law of Least Effort,* is based on the fact that nature's intelligence functions with effortless ease, with carefreeness, harmony, and love. This is the principle of "Do less, and accomplish more." When we learn this lesson from nature, we easily fulfill our desires.

If we observe nature at work, we see that the least effort is expended. Grass doesn't try to grow; it just grows. Fish don't try to swim; they just swim. This is their intrinsic nature. It is the nature of the sun to shine. And it is human nature to make our dreams manifest into physical form — easily and effortlessly. What is commonly called a "miracle" is actually an expression of the *Law of Least Effort*.

Least effort is expended when our actions are motivated by love, because nature is held together by the energy of love. When we seek power and control over other people, we spend energy in a wasteful way. When we seek money for personal gain only, we cut off the flow of energy to ourselves, and interfere with the expression of nature's intelligence.

We waste our energy chasing the illusion of happiness, instead of enjoying happiness in the moment. Attention to the whims of the ego consumes the greatest amount of energy. But when our internal reference point is our spirit, our actions are motivated by love, and there is no waste of energy. Our energy multiplies, and the surplus energy we gather can be channeled to create anything we want, including unlimited wealth. When we harness the power of harmony and love, we use our energy creatively for the experience of affluence and evolution.

❧

How can you put the *Law of Least Effort* into action? There are three things you can do.

The first thing is to accept people, situations, and events as they *are*, not as you *wish* they were, in this moment. This moment is as it should be, because it took the entire universe to make this moment. When you struggle against this moment, you struggle against the entire universe. You can *intend* for things to be different in the future, but in *this* moment, accept things as they are.

The second thing is to take responsibility for your situation and for all the events you see as problems. This means not blaming anyone or anything for your situation, including yourself. Responsibility means the *ability* to have a creative response to the situation *as it is now*. All problems contain the seeds of opportunity, and this awareness allows you to take the moment and transform it into a better situation.

If you do this, every upsetting situation becomes an opportunity for the creation of something new and beautiful; every tormentor or tyrant becomes your teacher. The relationships you have attracted in your life are precisely the ones you need at this moment; there is a hidden meaning behind all events that is serving your own evolution. And if you choose to interpret reality in this way, then you will have many teachers and many opportunities to evolve.

A third way to put the *Law of Least Effort* into action is to practice defenselessness. This means relinquishing the need to convince others of your point of view. By doing this, you gain access to enormous amounts of energy that have previously been wasted.

When you have no point to defend, you stop fighting and resisting, and you can fully experience the present, which is a gift. When you embrace the present, you begin to experience the spirit within everything that is alive, and joy is born within you. As you drop the burden of defensiveness and resentment, you become lighthearted, joyous, and free. In this joyful, simple freedom, you will know that what you want is available to you whenever you want it, because your want is coming from a state of happiness, not from a state of anxiety and fear.

The *Law of Least Effort* assures us that there is always a simple, natural path to fulfillment.

Nature's intelligence unfolds spontaneously through the path of least effort and no resistance. This is the way that you can live, too. When you combine acceptance, responsibility, and defenselessness, your life flows with effortless ease. Your dreams and desires flow with nature's desires. Then you can release your intentions without attachment, and when the season is right, your desires will blossom into reality.

To experience the *Law of Least Effort*:

❖ Accept people, circumstances, and events as they are in this moment. When confronted with any challenge, remind yourself, *"This moment is as it should be,"* because the entire universe is as it should be.

❖ Take responsibility for your situation without blaming anything or anyone, including yourself. Every problem is an opportunity to take this moment and transform it into a greater benefit.

❖ Relinquish the need to defend your point of view. In defenselessness, you remain open to all points of view, not rigidly attached to one of them.

# 5

❧

## THE LAW OF
## INTENTION AND DESIRE

*In the beginning there was desire, which*
*was the first seed of mind. . . .*
*— Hymn of Creation, The Rig Veda*

# 5

# THE LAW OF
# INTENTION AND DESIRE

The fifth spiritual law of success, the *Law of Intention and Desire*, says that our intentions and desires, when released in the field of pure potentiality, have infinite organizing power. Just by introducing an intention in the fertile ground of pure potentiality, we activate this field, and put its infinite organizing power to work for us. This isn't a mystical notion. Every time we have a desire to walk or lift our arms, our intention incites millions of chemical reactions and electrical impulses that obey fixed laws of nature. The fifth spiritual law says that inherent in every desire are the mechanics for its fulfillment, and these mechanics apply to desires reaching far beyond the physical body.

Energy and information exist everywhere in nature; at the level of pure consciousness, there is nothing other than energy and information. This means there are no well-defined edges between our physical body and our extended body — the universe. We can consciously change the energy and information of our *own* body, and influence the energy and information of our *extended* body — our environment — and cause things to manifest in it.

This change is brought about by two qualities inherent in consciousness: attention and intention. Attention energizes, and intention transforms. Whatever we put our attention on grows stronger in our life; whatever we take our attention away from withers and disappears. Intention triggers the transformation of energy and information, and organizes its own fulfillment. The quality of *intention* on the object of *attention* orchestrates an infinity of details to bring about the intended outcome.

We see the expression of this organizing power in every blade of grass, in every flower, in everything that is alive. In the scheme of nature, everything is connected and correlated with everything else. The groundhog comes out of the earth, and we know it is going to be spring. Birds begin to migrate in a certain direction at a certain time of the year. Nature is a symphony that is silently orchestrated at the ultimate ground of creation. As long as we do not violate the other laws of nature, we can use conscious intent to literally command the powers of nature to fulfill our dreams and desires.

Intention is the real power behind desire because it is desire *without attachment* to the outcome. Desire in most people is attention with attachment to the outcome. But when we combine intention with detachment, our *intent* is for the future, while our *attention* is in the present. Present-moment awareness is powerful, because the future is created by our actions in the present. We cannot take action in the past or in the future. Past and future are born in the imagination. Only the present, which is awareness, is real and eternal.

If we practice present-moment awareness, then the imaginary obstacles — which are more than 90 percent of the obstacles — disappear. The remaining obstacles can be transformed into opportunities through one-pointed intention. This means holding our attention to the intended outcome with such unbending purpose that we refuse to allow obstacles to consume our attention, or to

dissipate the focused quality of our attention. This is the power of focused intention
and detachment simultaneously.

❦

How can you harness the power of intention
to fulfill your dreams and desires? You can
get results through effort, but if you follow
these five steps in the *Law of Intention and
Desire*, your intention will generate its own
power: 1) Center yourself in the silent space
between thoughts — in the essential state of
*Being*; 2) Release your intentions and desires
with the expectation that they will bloom
when the season is right; 3) Keep your
desires to yourself; do not share them with
anyone else unless they are closely bonded

with you; 4) Relinquish your attachment to the outcome; and 5) Let the universe handle the details.

Remember, your true nature is one of pure potentiality. You don't need to look at yourself through the eyes of the world, or allow yourself to be influenced by the opinions of others. Remain established in the awareness of your *true* Self. Carry the awareness of your spirit wherever you go, gently release your desires, and the universe will orchestrate all the details for you.

To experience the *Law of Intention and Desire*:

❖ Make a list of your intentions and desires, and look at this list before you go into silence, before you go to sleep at night, and when you wake up in the morning.

❖ Release your desires to the field of pure potentiality, trusting it to handle all the details for you. Know that when things don't seem to go your way, there is a reason.

❖ Practice present-moment awareness in all your actions. Refuse to allow obstacles to consume your attention in the present moment.

# 6

## THE LAW OF
## DETACHMENT

*The ego and the Self dwell in the same body.*
*The former eats the sweet and sour fruits of the tree*
*of life, while the latter looks on in detachment.*
*— Mundaka Upanishad*

# 6

# THE LAW OF
# DETACHMENT

The sixth spiritual law of success, the *Law of Detachment*, says that the way to acquire anything in the universe is to relinquish our attachment to it. This doesn't mean we give up the intention to create our desire; we don't give up the intention, and we don't give up the desire. We give up our attachment to the outcome. The moment we combine one-pointed intention with detachment to the outcome, we will have that which we desire.

Anything we want can be acquired through detachment, because detachment is based on the unquestioning belief in the power of the Self. The source of wealth — or of anything in the physical world — is the Self, the field of pure potentiality that knows how to manifest everything. All we need to do is nurture our deepest intentions in our heart and go with the flow.

Detachment comes from an inner knowingness that we are a pattern of behavior of a higher intelligence. When things don't seem to go our way, we can let go of our idea of how things should be. We know that in our limited awareness, we cannot see the synchronistic, harmonious patterns of the universe of which we and our intentions are a part.

Attachment, on the other hand, implies doubt and distrust in nature's intelligence and its infinite organizing power. Attachment is the melodrama of the ego, because it is based on fear and insecurity, and this comes from not realizing the power of the Self. Those who seek security chase it for a lifetime without ever finding it, because security can never come from material wealth alone. People say, "When I have a million dollars, then I'll be financially independent; then I'll be secure." But it never happens. Attachment to money and security only creates insecurity, no matter how much money we have in the bank.

Attachment to the symbols of wealth — cars, houses, bank notes — creates anxiety because the symbols are transitory; they come and go. When we exchange our Self for the *symbols* of our Self, we end up feeling empty inside.

The search for security is actually an attachment to certainty, to the known, and the known is the prison of our past conditioning. Freedom from our past lies in the wisdom of *uncertainty*. Without uncertainty, life is just the repetition of outworn memories. There's no evolution in that, and when there is no evolution, there is stagnation, entropy, and decay.

In ancient wisdom traditions, the solution to this dilemma lies in our willingness to detach from the known, step into the unknown, and surrender our desires to the creative mind that orchestrates the dance of the universe. The unknown is the field of all possibilities, ever fresh, ever new, always open to the creation of new manifestations. This field can orchestrate an infinity of space-time events to bring about the outcome intended. But when our intention gets locked into a rigid mindset, we lose the fluidity, flexibility, and creativity inherent in the field.

Attachment to a specific outcome freezes our desire into a rigid framework, and this interferes with the whole process of creation.

True wealth consciousness is the ability to have anything we want, anytime we want, with the least effort. Detachment is synonymous with wealth consciousness, because with detachment there is freedom to create. How can we create when we're clinging and grasping, and full of anxiety? We don't need to have a complete and rigid idea of what we'll be doing next week or next year, because if we get rigidly attached to that idea, then we shut out a whole range of possibilities.

The *Law of Detachment* does not interfere with goal setting. We still have the intention of going in a certain direction, but between point A and point B there are infinite possibilities. With uncertainty factored in, we might change direction if we find a higher ideal, or if we find something more exciting. When we experience uncertainty, we're on the right path, and it's the fertile ground of pure creativity and freedom.

How can you apply the *Law of Detachment?* Begin by practicing detached involvement. This means whenever you encounter a problem, you stay grounded in the wisdom of uncertainty, while expectantly waiting for a solution to emerge. If you remain detached, you won't feel compelled to force solutions on problems. This enables you to stay alert to opportunities, and then what emerges is something powerful and exciting. The state of alert preparedness in the present meets with your goals and intentions, and allows you to seize the opportunity within every problem you have in your life.

Every problem is the seed of an opportunity for some greater benefit. Once you have this perception, a whole range of possibilities opens up, and this keeps the wonder and the excitement alive. Only by practicing detached involvement can you have joy and laughter. Then wealth is created spontaneously and effortlessly.

The word *universe* means one song. Your every intention or heart's desire is like a melody in nature's symphony; all you have to do is sing your song. A Rumi poem says, "I want to sing like birds sing, not worrying who listens or what they think." If you can sing your song with that attitude, you are participating in the *Law of Detachment*, and nothing will be able to stop the force of your intentions.

Relinquish your attachment to the known, step into the unknown, and experience all the fun, mystery, and magic of what may occur in the field of all possibilities. When your preparedness meets opportunity, a solution will spontaneously appear that benefits you and all those around you.

What is commonly called "good luck" is nothing but preparedness and opportunity coming together. This is the perfect recipe for success, and it is based on the *Law of Detachment*.

To experience the *Law of Detachment:*

❖ Practice detached involvement. Stay alert to the opportunity within every problem by letting go of your idea of how things should be.

❖ Accept uncertainty as an essential part of your experience. In your willingness to accept uncertainty, solutions will spontaneously appear.

❖ Remain open to all possibilities and enjoy every moment in the journey of your life — all the fun, mystery, and magic in the field of pure potentiality.

# 7

## THE LAW OF DHARMA
## OR PURPOSE IN LIFE

*To work with love... is to weave the cloth with threads drawn from your heart, even as if your beloved were to wear that cloth.*
— Kahlil Gibran, The Prophet

# 7

# The Law of Dharma
# or Purpose in Life

The seventh spiritual law of success, the *Law of Dharma* or *Purpose in Life*, says that we are spiritual beings who have taken physical form to fulfill a purpose. Everyone has a purpose in life — a unique gift or special talent to give to others, and for every unique talent and expression of that talent, there are also unique needs. When we blend this unique talent with service to others, we experience the ecstasy and exultation of our spirit. This is the goal of all goals.

There are three components to the *Law of Dharma*. The first component says that each of us is here to discover our true Self, to find out that we are spiritual beings, or divinity in disguise.

The second component of the *Law of Dharma* says that each of us has a unique talent that we are here to express. Our talent is so unique that no one else alive has that talent, or that expression of that talent. When we are expressing our unique talent — or more than one talent in many cases — we are happy, and we lose track of time.

The third component of the *Law of Dharma* says that we are here to serve our fellow human beings with our talent. By asking the question "How can I help all those with whom I come into contact?" we combine the expression of our unique talent with service to humanity, and make full use of the *Law of Dharma*.

The experience of our spirituality, coupled with the expression of our talent in service to humanity gives us access to unlimited abundance. This is the spark that generates abundance, and it's permanent, not temporary, because this is the *real* way abundance is achieved. By asking the question "How can I help?" instead of "What's in it for me?" we go beyond the internal dialogue

of the ego, into the domain of our spirit —
that part of our awareness where we experience our universality.

The *Law of Dharma* implies more than
seeking work that we love; it implies our
unique destiny, our place in the cosmic
plan. It implies a shift in consciousness that
begins when we align ourselves with our
highest vision, and then become the manifestation of that vision. The force that serves
as a bridge to such a transformation is also
known as dharma.

First comes the moment when we realize
that life cannot succeed without a vision.
Then we arrive at the biggest mystery of
all. What is the meaning of our lives in the
scheme of the universe? The root of the word

*dharma*, in Sanskrit, gives us a valuable clue: It means "to uphold." We know we've become part of the cosmic plan when the universe upholds and supports us. The seventh spiritual law of success brings the preceding six laws to fruition, for when we master the *Law of Dharma*, the whole universe is on our side. Every law and power of nature comes to our aid and supports us spontaneously.

Self-exploration isn't a task we accomplish and then abandon. Every person is a never-ending project of the universe. We are like ships in the night, and the current that holds us up and carries us toward the dawn is dharma. If we open our spiritual eyes and see through the illusion of our conditioning, then the path of dharma beckons us. It was there all along. It is there now, at this very moment, calling out from the depths of our own awareness.

❧

If you want to experience the *Law of Dharma*, there are several things you can do. The first is to seek your higher Self through spiritual practice and discover your divinity; the second is to find your unique talents; and the third is to serve humanity with the expression of your talents.

If money was no concern and you had all the time in the world, what would you do? If you would still do what you currently do, then you are in dharma because you have passion for what you do. How are you best suited to serve humanity? Answer that question, put it into practice, and you can generate all the wealth that you want.

When your creative expressions match the needs of your fellow humans, wealth spontaneously flows from the realm of the spirit to the world of form. You begin to experience your life as a miraculous expression of divinity — not just occasionally, but all the time. And you will know true joy and the true meaning of success — the ecstasy and exultation of your own spirit.

To experience the *Law of Dharma*:

❖ Nurture the divinity within you, the spirit animating your body and mind, by carrying the consciousness of timeless *Being* in the midst of time-bound experience.

❖ Make a list of your unique talents. Then list all the things that you love to do while expressing these talents.

❖ Ask yourself daily, "How can I help?" and "How can I serve?" The answers to these questions will help you to serve your fellow human beings with love.

*Manifest the divinity within you, and everything*
*will be harmoniously arranged around it.*
— *Swami Vivekananda*

## AFTERWORD

The universal mind choreographs everything that is happening in billions of
galaxies with elegant precision and unfalter-
ing intelligence. Its intelligence permeates
every fiber of existence — from the atom to
the cosmos. And this intelligence operates
through the seven spiritual laws.

When we put our attention on these laws and practice the steps outlined in this book, we can manifest anything we want — all the affluence and success that we desire. Life becomes more joyful and abundant in every way, for these laws are also the spiritual laws of life that make living worthwhile.

Everything in life is an expression of the miraculous unfolding of spirit. In every moment, spirit just unfolds spontaneously, and the universe evolves into higher levels of creativity, awareness, and divinity.

True success is to witness the unfolding of the divinity within us. It is the perception of divinity wherever we go, in whatever we perceive — in the eyes of a child, in the beauty of a flower, in the flight of a bird.

When we experience every moment of our lives as the miraculous expression of divinity, then we'll know the true meaning of success.

We are travelers on a cosmic journey, and this moment is a little parenthesis in eternity. Life is eternal, but the expressions of life are momentary and transient. Buddha once said, "This existence of ours is as transient as autumn clouds. . . . A lifetime is like a flash of lightning in the sky, rushing by like a torrent down a steep mountain."

We have stopped for a moment to encounter one another, to meet, to love, to share. If we share with caring, lightheartedness, and love, we will create abundance and joy for one another. And then this moment will have been worthwhile.

Deepak Chopra is a world-renowned leader in the fields of holistic health and human potential, and the international bestselling author of numerous books and audio programs that cover every aspect of mind, body, and spirit. His books have been translated into more than fifty languages, and he travels widely throughout the world promoting peace, health, and well-being.

For a complete list of books and audio programs by Deepak Chopra, or for information about ongoing seminars, lectures, and special events at The Chopra Center at La Costa Resort and Spa in Carlsbad, California, please visit Deepak's website at:

www.deepakchopra.com

*The Seven Spiritual Laws of Success DVD*
Featuring Deepak Chopra and singer Olivia Newton-John, this compelling DVD intertwines Chopra's essential teachings with the personal stories of people who have used the seven spiritual laws to transform their lives. Available at major bookstores, DVD retailers, or online at www.hayhouse.com.

*The Seven Spiritual Laws of Success*
Available in unabridged hardcover edition, and in audiobook (read by the author).

*Creating Affluence*
Chopra explores the full meaning of wealth consciousness, and presents a series of A-to-Z steps that generate wealth in all its forms.

*Power, Freedom, and Grace*

Deepak Chopra considers the mystery of our existence, and its significance in our eternal quest for happiness. *Who am I? Where did I come from? Where do I go when I die?* Chopra draws upon the ancient philosophy of Vedanta and the findings of modern science to help us understand and experience our true nature.

❧

For a free catalog of Amber-Allen books and audios, please contact:

Amber-Allen Publishing

P. O. Box 6657

San Rafael, CA 94903-0657

(800) 624-8855

Visit us online: www.amberallen.com